# This Book Belongs To

______________________________

Made in the USA
Monee, IL
20 May 2022

96723720R00061